Foresight

Foresight

*Leadership Lessons for the
21st Century*

Alan G. Vitters

outskirts
press

Foresight
Leadership Lessons for the 21st Century
All Rights Reserved.
Copyright © 2023 Alan G. Vitters
v2.0

The opinions expressed in this manuscript are solely the opinions of the author and do not represent the opinions or thoughts of the publisher. The author has represented and warranted full ownership and/or legal right to publish all the materials in this book.

This book may not be reproduced, transmitted, or stored in whole or in part by any means, including graphic, electronic, or mechanical without the express written consent of the publisher except in the case of brief quotations embodied in critical articles and reviews.

Outskirts Press, Inc.
http://www.outskirtspress.com

Paperback ISBN: 978-1-9772-5852-6
Hardback ISBN: 978-1-9772-5934-9

Library of Congress Control Number: 2022921551

Copyright Registration Number TXu 2-337-726

Cover Photo © 2023 www.gettyimages.com. All rights reserved - used with permission.

Outskirts Press and the "OP" logo are trademarks belonging to Outskirts Press, Inc.

PRINTED IN THE UNITED STATES OF AMERICA

Dedication

To Katherine and Scott

And

Generations of Students for Their

Meaningful Insights

Acknowledgments

I would like to acknowledge the contribution to the creation of this book by the dedicated and professional staff at Outskirts Press- Deni Sinterai-Scott, Alanna Boutin, and Pat Wilson.

I would also like to recognize the following individuals who greatly influenced my awareness and appreciation for the subject matter of "FORESIGHT" about which I am passionate- George Odiorne, Arben Clark, Fred Herzberg, Gerard Carvalho, Oakley Gordon, Joe Bentley, Martin Chemers and countless friends, colleagues, and influencers from the profession of arms.

Thank-you.

Foreword

This is a book about concepts, theories, cases, and examples that derive from the social and behavioral sciences that relate to being an effective leader in the 21st century. Some of the insights are classical, and some are cutting-edge and modern.

This book is designed for leaders in all walks of life—business, the military, first responders, and other service-oriented volunteers and workers. It is written for first-line supervisors, middle managers, and executives. Hopefully, with foresight and determination, you can succeed and make a difference in your organization.

Many traits could be highlighted as relevant to leadership—drive, stamina, perseverance, and intuition, to name a few. However, the author has decided to focus on one seldomly cited trait—*foresight*. Foresight is developed through intentional study and practice—hands-on application and experience. Foresight enables someone to face new issues and challenges with confidence and a feeling of "having seen this before."

Much of the content of this book derives from the author's own journey as a military leader and educator to prepare himself as an aspiring leader with knowledge and to reflect on lessons learned the hard way . . . through trial and error.

No one is ever fully equipped to be an effective leader at the outset, but it's essential to get "into the arena" and to do one's best. Leadership is truly a "come as you are" process.

Contents

Acknowledgments	i
Foreword	iii
PART ONE: INDIVIDUAL COMPETENCE	**1**
1 Management Basics	3
Essay: "The Essence of Management"	5
Essay: "Evaluating Evaluations—Another Look"	7
2 Problem-Solving and Decision-Making	9
Essay: One-Minute Manager—Decision-Making	11
3 Emotional Intelligence (EI)	14
Essay: "Emotional Intelligence in Schools"	16
4 Leadership	17
Essay: "Leadership in the Future: The 'Androgynous' Leader"	20
5 Motivation	22
Essay: "Motivation"	24

6	Stress	28
7	Learning	30
	Essay: "Positive Psychology and the PSYCAP Model"	33

PART TWO: GROUP PROCESSES — 35

1	High-Performing Teams	37
	Essay: "Teamwork and Synchronization: The 'Blitzkrieg' of the '80s"	40
2	Diversity and Multigenerational Teams	50
	Essay: "The <u>Sense of a Goose</u>"	53

PART THREE: ORGANIZATION DYNAMICS — 55

1	Strategy	57
	Essay: "Open-Systems: Ignore at Your Peril"	60
	Essay: "Paradigms"	62
2	Organization Culture	64
3	Organization Development/Effectiveness (OD/OE)	67
	Essay: "Organization Dynamics in the Future"	69
	Essay: "Organization Change and Development"	72
4	Organization Conflict and Innovation	81
	Essay: "Innovation—The Nuthatch Way"	83
5	Ethics and Social Responsibility	84
	Essay: "Professional Ethics—Briefly Noted"	87
6	Organization Design	90
	References	92
	About the Author	96

Part One:
INDIVIDUAL COMPETENCE

1

Management Basics

"Perfection Is the Enemy of the Good"
—*Anonymous*

Achieving excellent outcomes in any organization—business, the military, academia, the government—can either be managed or left to chance. The better choice is managing to be efficient and effective.

At its core, management is functions like planning, organizing, leading, and controlling. It consists of theory, concepts, terms, models, and, most importantly, practice and experience.

The theory of management thought has evolved from ancient Egypt, China, and Europe to the West's Industrial Revolution and our modern computer-driven era. Different schools of management thought grew from scientific management, general administrative theory, human relations, quantitative emphasis, and statistics to contingency-based concepts.

Managers today face many issues in supervising and leading others

FORESIGHT

in the 21st century. Some of these issues are the rise of social media platforms, political polarization, security concerns, globalization, health pandemics (like COVID-19), workforce diversity, and the impact of morale and the "great resignation."

In completing its basic tasks or functions, managers need to be cognizant of a changing landscape. In planning, managers need conceptual and cognitive skills in using the many analytic, computer-based tools available. In addition to short (1–3 year) and long (3+ year) plans, contingency plans are important to address a rapidly changing technological environment. In organizing, managers need to be adaptable and flexible in "matching" people to tasks. The organization chart visually depicting hierarchical relationships needs to be continuously analyzed to create the best structure to accommodate current needs. Finally, leadership skills must be "developed" in managers to be effective in different situations. Traditional command and control styles, appropriate in some situations, may need to be supplemented with more people-oriented styles that rely on trust, cooperation, and relationships.

Control continues to be an important managerial function. Systems like budgeting controls, balanced scorecards, progress made on goals and objectives, and workplace security and surveillance measures must be overseen, monitored, adjusted, and fixed to guarantee efficiency and effectiveness.

(See the essays "The Essence of Management" and "Evaluating Evaluations—Another Look.")

ESSAY:
"THE ESSENCE OF MANAGEMENT"

I have been interested in the theory and practice of management for over 40-plus years. So what is it that truly separates a great, high-performing manager from the one that most of us have had to work for? After considerable reflection and some valuable insights from others over the years, I think it comes down to five essential ingredients. This is what all effective managers do.

1. **Clarify Expectations**

First, they tell the people who work for them what they expect them to do. Many managers "manage by mystery." That is, they keep you guessing about what you're supposed to contribute. The danger is that you might find yourself downsized or dismissed someday without ever seeing it coming.

2. **Provide Resources**

Second, effective managers give you the tools you need to accomplish the job. Managers are supposed to provide you with the equipment, people, funds, and time you will need to accomplish the task. Beware of the just "make it happen" folks who often rely on pressure and aloofness to get results on the cheap, and at *your* expense.

3. **Stay Off Their Back**

Third, managers must give associates the flexibility and space they need to get the job done. Few of us like working for a micromanager who personally intervenes in the process of doing a job. In other words, tell people "what to do, not how to do it."

4. Provide Feedback

Fourth, counseling and coaching are critical skills of effective managers. Feedback should be specific, timely, relevant, and helpful to get the job done. A very successful soccer coach I had in college said, "feedback is the breakfast of champions." (His teams got to the Division 1, NCAA Final Four for three years in a row.)

5. Reward When Deserved

Fifth, good managers reward people for their outstanding results. This can be as simple as verbal praise, which, in my view, is used too infrequently, or more elaborate recognition. B. F. Skinner, the father of learning theory, noted that "behavior is a function of its consequences." To be effective, it's important to be skilled at managing the contingencies found in the workplace.

If all managers learned to manage by following the above five essential principles, we would see many more world-class, high-performing outfits.

ESSAY: "EVALUATING EVALUATIONS— ANOTHER LOOK"

A great deal has been in Long Island newspapers lately about evaluating teachers. It seems to be an emotional topic since a quick word search of "school evaluations" reveals words like "unsettling," "toxic," and "problematic." So I thought it might be helpful to offer some insights on the subject from the perspective of how "performance evaluation (or appraisal)" is addressed in the business school classroom.

First and foremost, all performance evaluation systems should be focused on evaluation *and* development. They should be evaluative to help sort out performance levels—high performers from average or low performers. Then when it comes time to discriminate between individuals for the purpose of bonuses, merit pay, and even verbal praise, there needs to be some objective performance data in place.

The other purpose of evaluation methods should be to *develop* individuals. People need feedback and time to improve and practice new skills. Therefore, one of the most important roles of any supervisor is to motivate, counsel, and develop their teams or direct reports. This is a vital function of any evaluation system.

One organizational strategy that has proved particularly effective is an intervention called "management by objectives (MBO)." To quote the late George Odiorne, a former student of Peter Drucker and one of the early pioneers of MBO, "it is a process whereby the supervisor (department chair in the public-school example) and direct reports (teachers) jointly identify their common objectives, define each individual's major areas of responsibility in terms of the results expected, and use these measures as guides for operating the organization and assessing the contribution of its members." This is primarily done through collaborative meetings, periodic (quarterly) performance counseling, and through the preparation of a final audit—the annual performance report (Odiorne 1965, p. 55).

This kind of strategy, which is most often used in corporate America, the military, and occasionally in government, seems to be most successful where lots of performance data exist. Most schools routinely collect lots of data of this kind—test scores, attendance and graduation statistics, classroom evaluations, etc. End-of-year evaluations should be based on many objective (numerical data) and subjective measures, and no single measure (like test scores) should be used alone.

It is undoubtedly true that unionized, public school environments pose a challenge for such a system to succeed, but by focusing on the central pillars of continuous improvement, empowerment of teachers (through collaborative, objective setting), constant feedback, and a laser like focus on student learning and achievement, resistance and barriers can be overcome.

2

Problem-Solving and Decision-Making

*"Don't put off until tomorrow
what you can delegate today"*
—*Facella*

One of the most essential skills of effective managers is the ability to solve problems. A Rand study of "successful" officers found this to be the most critical skill to possess. In decision-making, it can be beneficial to follow models for problem-solving. The most well-known and frequently used is the Rational or Dewey problem-solving model. However, other approaches, like the Carnegie, Incremental, Unstructured, and Garbage Can models, can be used. All of these can be helpful in different situations. These are discussed in more detail in the Essay—"One-Minute Manager—Decision Making."

Managers tend to have different styles of making decisions. The *Directive* style tends to use minimal information and considers few alternatives. These tend to be intuitive managers who rely heavily on their own judgment and experience and focus on "seat of the pants" or gut methods. One example might be former President Trump, according to reports. Another style is the *Analytic*, where managers make decisions after extensive reviews of data and facts related to a problem. Former President Obama might be an example. Related to the Analytic approach is the *Conceptual*, where decisions are guided by theory, concepts, and reviews of the relevant literature. Dr. Tony Fauci comes to mind in combating COVID-19. The last approach is the *Behavioral*, which relies heavily on brainstorming, consensus building, and group activity. Former President Johnson in seeking compromise and input from all stakeholders is an example.

There are many guidelines or habits to consider when attempting to improve your decision-making process. These include attempts to understand cultural differences; recognize the time may come to cease attempts to solve intractable problems; defer to experts on the front line; embrace complexity and ambiguity; beware of being tricked by your own success. It also includes learning to listen; convert attempts (or trials) into "learning opportunities" (especially when things go wrong); experiment and pilot alternative courses of action; make use of gaming and simulations; use cross-functional teams for analyzing alternatives; and foster a culture that encourages risk taking and experimentation.

(See the essay "One-Minute Manager—Decision-Making.")

ESSAY: ONE-MINUTE MANAGER— DECISION-MAKING

In any organization—business, military, academic, or health care—decision-making is one of the most critical processes. For example, in a Rand study of "successful" army officers, defined as having been promoted to general officer rank, a question was asked: "To what skills or abilities did they attribute their success?" The most frequently cited ability was being an effective problem-solver/decision-maker.

In management literature, several different models of decision-making are found. Among the models are the Rational, Carnegie, Incremental, Unstructured, and Garbage Can models. A brief description follows.

In the *Rational* model, often called the "Dewey Problem-Solving Model," the steps are: (1) to define the problem—often viewed as the gap between actual and desired outcomes, (2) to collect data and information related to the issue, (3) to develop courses of action or alternative solutions, (4) to select one alternative and implement it, and (5) to evaluate the outcome. It should be noted that many people/organizations are good at analyzing problems but not so good at implementing/executing them. Execution is a critical step and often is enhanced by experience and "trial and error." The Rational model is probably the most often used in most organizations. It is very important that the last step of the model, evaluation, not be overlooked. Often, a "pilot" project of possible alternatives is helpful to see results achieved, or not, using a smaller population before going all-in and committing substantial financial resources. One must also ensure not to rush the process, lest failure ensues by doing "business at the speed of stupid"—the title of a bestselling book (Simon 1960).

The next model is the *Carnegie* model. This process is all about compromise, which is often referred to as the "Congressional model," although there hasn't been much compromise of late in that body. This model usually requires "satisficing" or adopting a less-than-perfect solution but one that is practically achievable and acceptable to all stakeholders (Larkey & Sproule, 1984, pp.1–8).

The third model is the *Incremental* model. This is when decision-makers make minor adjustments over time in critical inputs or resources. Most often, these are increases in personnel or funds. The strategy used in fighting the Vietnam War by decision-makers is an example of incrementalism, or gradualism. Small numbers of troops and funding in the early '60s gradually led to huge investments by the late '60s and early '70s. (Lindblom 1959, pp. 79–88).

The fourth model is the *Unstructured* model. In this instance, little is known about the problem at hand or even about alternatives to apply. Often, brainstorming and "thinking outside the box" analysis is used to develop creative, novel, and innovative solutions. An example of this might come from NASA, when a space capsule was damaged on launch, and creative ideas were needed to fix the damaged panels to allow for a safe reentry. A catastrophe was averted by soliciting feedback and input worldwide on potential solutions (Mintzberg, Raisinghani & Theoret 1976, pp. 246–275).

The last model is the *Garbage Can* model. In this case, a solution is known to the problem, but there is a need for additional information on the nature of the problem itself or who might most benefit. An example might derive from a hospital setting where there has been a significant investment in new surgical equipment technology. Still, the people to most benefit from it must be identified. For example, hospitals investing in cutting-edge prostate cancer technology and proton beam devices must find the patients that will benefit most (Cohen, March & Olson 1972, pp.1–25).

The most applicable model to army practitioners is probably the Rational model. Units of all branches and sizes routinely address problems that are negatively affecting unit readiness and effectiveness. Following a structured plan of analysis and then effectively implementing a course of action and evaluating the outcome is smart leadership.

3

Emotional Intelligence (EI)

"EQ is More Important than IQ"

—*Goleman*

Daniel Goleman has written extensively about the concept of "Emotional Intelligence." A core principle that has been supported by his research is that Emotional Quotient (EQ) is as important to developing one's potential as Intelligence Quotient (IQ). In his writing, Goleman notes that Emotional Intelligence is essentially having a good "bedside manner" (Goleman 1998, p.11).

Goleman notes that people have personal and social competencies to varying levels that impact their personality. In his early work, he highlighted the following as personal competencies: self-awareness, self-regulation, and motivation. Social competencies focused on empathy and social skills. In more recent research, he has noted the importance of social awareness and relationship management to social competence. His insight on human behavior and what it takes to be an effective leader and manager is most valuable

(Goleman 1998, pp. 26–27).

Self-awareness can be improved by taking many inventories, instruments, and tests developed by social and behavioral scientists over the years. A few personal favorites are the "Learning Style Inventory" (Kolb), "Career Anchors" (Schein), "Myers-Briggs Inventory" (Myers-Briggs), and the US Army's "Armed Services Vocational Aptitude Battery" (ASVAB). These are excellent tools for learning more about yourself and matching your personal interests to vocational, occupational, and professional positions and careers.

(See the essay "Emotional Intelligence in Schools.")

ESSAY: "EMOTIONAL INTELLIGENCE IN SCHOOLS"

Much has been written about the importance of "intelligence" (and IQ) in predicting success in later life. There is also a growing body of literature about the importance of "emotional intelligence" (or EQ) in shaping one's later success.

The author, Daniel Goleman, has written a great deal about "emotional intelligence," which he refers to, for lack of better words, as having good "bedside manners." To Goleman, the central elements of emotional intelligence are "self-awareness, self-regulation, motivation, empathy, and social skills." The mastery of these behaviors separates the truly high performers from the rest of the pack in careers (Goleman 1998, pp. 26–27).

A relevant question then is, what are we doing to develop these skills, attitudes, and behaviors in our young folks today? Not too long ago, I heard a past secretary of education note the importance of EI in a speech to educators. In addition, he challenged the audience to explore innovative ways to teach EI and its principles in our schools.

In the news, we read a lot about the prevalence of bullying, poor manners, incivility, and fighting in our schools and workplaces—even the NFL. Perhaps a good place to start in reversing these trends is in providing training in EI to our school and workplace employees.

4

Leadership

"Leadership—It Depends on the Situation."
—Anonymous

Most people agree that leadership is a process to influence others to achieve a goal. Influence often derives from having a vision and inspiring others to accomplish it. Leadership differs from management in that it is a very people-oriented process that is both an art and a science. After considerable research, over decades, it is encouraging to know that leadership skills *can* be taught. Although there is a relationship between difficult characteristics to change, like height, image, and personality traits, much can be learned about becoming a better leader through seminars, exercises, podcasts, and reading. There are many valuable approaches to gaining leadership insights by analyzing traits, principles, concepts, and theories.

Traits are generally aspects of one's personality and can be useful in being an effective leader. Some common leadership traits are courage, intelligence, humility, perseverance, empathy, and determination. In the future, leaders will need to be adaptable and draw on "foresight" to be more effective.

There are many valuable concepts and theories on leadership that come from social and behavioral research. For example, research has shown that there are basically two styles of leadership. They go by somewhat different names but relate to "task-oriented" and "people-oriented." Leaders with task styles are best at organizing, using performance metrics, and monitoring goal and objective progress. People-oriented leaders tend to focus more on coaching, mentoring, communicating, and affirming the contributions of others. Many theories of leadership have been developed, including the "Managerial Grid" (Blake and Mouton), the "Situational Model" (Hersey and Blanchard), and the "Contingency Model" (Fiedler). All these examine the relationship between leader styles, the situation- in terms of the task at hand and follower characteristics, and group performance or effectiveness. Two more recent models are "Servant Leadership" (an elegant concept) and "Toxic Leadership." Servant leaders emphasize authenticity and humility, turn the hierarchy upside down, and focus on vision, direction, and developing and growing their employees (Blanchard). Toxic leadership is characterized by leaders who put their own needs first, micromanage, are overly competitive, and often bully, demean, and lack self-control.

There are also leadership principles that can be insightful. The most well-known principle is to "lead by example." General Norman Schwarzkopf once explained this as "whenever your subordinates are doing something they don't want to do—do it with them." Examples of this might be working late on a project, under adverse conditions, or needing to perform tasks that are inherently dangerous but essential. Leadership author and practitioner Tom Kolditz has termed this phenomenon "leadership in extremis."

Although volumes have been written about leaders and leadership, relatively little has been written about followers. One of the first management theorists to do this was Mary Parker Follett. Her classic book, *Freedom and Coordination*, concluded that followers influence the leadership process in two ways. First, they can withhold effort to a task and only do what is required or stipulated in a job description. Second, followers could withhold critical information and feedback to perform a task successfully. In essence, like penguins, they would follow poor leaders off a cliff when they knew better. On the other hand, others have stated that followers can alter the situation if they work harder, speak positively about the organization, stay engaged and present (a significant factor in the "great resignation" era), and if they trust and fully share good and bad news (Follett 1933, pp. 47–60).

(See the essay "Leadership in the Future: The 'Androgynous' Leader.")

ESSAY:
"LEADERSHIP IN THE FUTURE: THE 'ANDROGYNOUS' LEADER"

In essence, leadership is the process of influencing human behavior to accomplish a goal. It involves an interaction between the leader and the led.

In studying leadership, most psychologists and social psychologists initially focused on traits. Traits are aspects of an individual's personality. For example, some traits most highly correlated with leadership effectiveness are integrity, honesty, moral courage, competence, and grit or perseverance.

The next phase of leadership research focused on "styles." It was noted that there are two basic styles of leadership: "task-oriented" and "relationship-oriented." People tend to emphasize one or the other in their approach to leading others.

More recently, leadership research has focused on the impact of the "situation" on the process. For example, is the situation chaotic or calm, how do the leaders and followers get along, is the task at hand structured, how much power does the leader have, and how much uncertainty exists in the environment?

It's interesting to look at the impact of gender on the leadership process. Research indicates that female leaders may be better at planning, coaching/counseling, communicating, and managing conflict. Male leaders tend to be better at decision-making and strategy. In classic research done at West Point in the 1970s when women were first admitted (Project Athena), there were far more similarities than differences found between these young leaders (Vitters and Kinzer 1977). Psychologically, men and women were similar, although some differences were found. There were significant physical differences found to exist, largely due to societal conditioning factors. Some interesting research suggests that women tend to be better managers/leaders than men since men tend to be more internally focused and women are more concerned with others and are therefore more externally focused.

It's interesting to contemplate the emergence of a new style of leadership—*the androgynous leader.* People may not be initially predisposed to this style but can become androgynous leaders—mainly through training. Androgynous leaders can assess a situation and exhibit the behaviors most suited to deal with the challenges effectively. This approach is not a stereotypically masculine or feminine style. It is a style defined by the process of assessing and analyzing and then drawing on a personal skill set (or tool kit) to select the right strategy or course of action to use. This process is analogous to that used by golfers in selecting the right club to use in a given situation based on the lie and distance required.

Androgynous Leadership—just a thought . . .

5

Motivation

"It's Efficient to Be Human"
—*Herzberg*

Undoubtedly, motivating associates is one of the most essential skills needed by all leaders/managers in all types of organizations. The word itself derives from the construct, "motive-action."

It is clear from research and practice that there is no "one best way" to motivate others. Motivation can come from factors within or without. There are many concepts and theories that are useful to practitioners and illuminate the subject. Two personal favorite theories are Herzberg's "Motivation-Hygiene Theory" and Vroom's "Expectancy Theory." In his book *Work and the Nature of Man* and his classic *Harvard Business Review* articles "One More Time—How Do You Motivate Your Employees" and "The Wise Old Turk," Herzberg's "content" theory identified the key factors that lead to "satisfaction" and "dissatisfaction" with employees. Factors that satisfied (the Motivators) were achievement, recognition, the work itself, responsibility, advancement, and growth. Factors that led to dissatisfaction (the Hygiene factors) were supervision, company policy, relationship with your supervisor, working conditions, SALARY, relationship with peers, personal life, status, and security. To Herzberg, organizations must build the Motivator factors into every job, a process he called "Job Enrichment" (Herzberg 1966, p. 73).

Victor Vroom is credited with a "process-centered" approach to motivation, which he called "Expectancy Theory." To Vroom, the way to motivate employees was to identify the outcomes/benefits that employees most desired, the strength of these (valence), and then ensure that if they worked hard and performed their tasks successfully, they would be generously compensated (instrumentality). This finding has led many modern companies and organizations to "tailor" their compensation packages to best meet the diverse needs of their employees (Vroom, 1964, pp. 17–18).

The most effective way to move from theory to practice is to do the following: use objectives (both individual and company), consider individual differences, use recognition and praise frequently, link rewards to performance, and ensure fair and equitable transactions.

In my experience, many "intangible" factors are seldom found in studies and texts that also influence motivation. Some of these are: a passion for a cause (an important factor to soldiers in war), to support or protect a "buddy" or other esteemed colleague, fear (students can be motivated to study to avoid a poor grade), pride, self-respect, and the pressure of time (burning the midnight oil to get that project done).

(See the essay "Motivation.")

ESSAY: "MOTIVATION"

(Source: initially published in *INFANTRY* magazine, Mar–Apr 1978.)

The army's ranks today are filled with men and women seeking an opportunity to grow and develop physically and mentally while in uniform. The army's ability to provide meaningful and challenging assignments for its young soldiers, both enlisted men and officers, may make the difference in whether the best of these are retained or lost to the army.

Because the army is really people—you and me—we must ask ourselves what we can do, as infantry leaders at the squad, company, and battalion levels, to help make the job of soldiering in a peacetime army a more meaningful and challenging experience for those below us.

The first thing we can do is to recognize and face up to the fact that motivating subordinates is, and will always be, an essential part of our jobs as leaders. Then we must try to get away from the negative notion that often accompanies the idea of motivation in the military services. A good example of that is shown by the following extract from an article that appeared in a 1969 issue of one of our leading news magazines:

"Rebels or laggards are sent to the Motivation Platoon to get 'squared away'. A day at 'Motivation' combines constant harassment and PT (physical training), ending the day with the infiltration course . . . At the end, the privates are lined up and asked if they are ready to go back to their home platoons . . . almost all go back for good."

Admittedly, this is one form of motivation that is probably effective in certain circumstances. But we need to recognize the existence of another form of motivation—the positive kind—that a leader at any level in the army hierarchy can use to help make a subordinate's job a more likely source of motivation for him. These are some of the more positive things a leader can do:

- *Tell his subordinates what's expected of them.* By so doing, the leader gives his subordinates objectives to work toward, which causes people to "stretch" on their jobs and can be the difference between making a job dull or challenging. All leaders must set clear objectives for their men and; in many instances, they can do this through their subordinates' active involvement and participation. Objectives make it possible for people to achieve, and achievement leads to motivation. Clear objectives also make possible clear and meaningful unit performance appraisals.

- *Provide the resources and support to accomplish the unit's mission.* There is no better way a leader can kill his subordinate's motivation than to fail to provide the necessary resources to do their jobs. What kind of motivation can be expected of a young noncommissioned officer who is told to train his squad when only half of his squad is ever present for training?

- *Stay off their backs.* This may be the most abused aspect of work in the army. For some reason, perhaps because of a lack of trust between leaders and subordinates, the leaders feel they must personally direct and control the efforts of those below them. The classic example of this could be observed on occasion in Vietnam where clusters of command-and-control helicopters congregated in the sky to direct a squad involved in a firefight in the jungle below. The word "trust" seems particularly relevant when used in this context.

- Close supervision, managerial controls, guarding, security, and sign-outs all carry with them, to some extent, the implication of distrust. Increasing evidence strongly suggests that distrusting people often becomes a self-confirming hypothesis in that distrust leads to behavior by those not trusted (consciously or unconsciously) designed to prove the validity of distrust. In other words, distrust begets distrust. The evidence also suggests that trust begets trust. When people are trusted, they often respond in ways to merit or justify that trust.

- Many of today's finest junior officers and noncommissioned officers were drawn to the army by what they saw as an opportunity to develop and use their leadership abilities in a meaningful way and in an atmosphere of trust. If the army is to retain these people, it must give them the opportunity to do so. In this regard, it also seems important to recognize that as individuals grow and develop as leaders, they will make errors. In fact, several authors have written that real growth is not possible without mistakes being made. One distinguished army officer has referred to this phenomenon as "the freedom to fail."

- *Provide feedback.* Here, leaders are called upon to employ all the counseling and interpersonal skills they should have acquired over the years. Although feedback can be given either in writing or orally, it appears that feedback given promptly, directly, orally, and in a non-evaluative manner is the most effective kind. Providing feedback, both positive and negative, is an integral part of any leader's job.

- *Reward exceptional performance.* Many learning theorists, such as Dr. B. F. Skinner, have written about the importance of using rewards and punishments to motivate and teach individuals. Of course, rewards are not the key to motivating subordinates. That distinction lies with the act of achieving an important goal itself. But they do provide a tool for leaders to use to recognize their subordinates' exceptional performances. Both rewards and punishments, though, must be used responsibly and wisely.

After all this, the question remains: what will *you* do to help make *your* subordinates' jobs more meaningful and challenging?

6

Stress

"Motivational Anxiety Is Good and Different than Stress"
—*Herzberg*

Twenty-first-century leaders need to recognize the stress that both they, and their associates, are often under. Stress can be viewed as the adverse reaction people have to excessive work demands and pressure. Stress is to be distinguished from what Herzberg called "motivational anxiety," which can be a positive contributor to high performance. So not all stress is bad, but too little of it can lead to apathy and disinterest. Too much can lead to dysfunction and burnout.

Stress has physical, psychological, and behavioral impacts. Physical symptoms can be hypertension, headaches, and adrenalin spikes. Psychological outcomes can be anxiety, disengagement, and tension. Behavioral impacts can be absenteeism, irritability, accidents, and misuse of drugs and alcohol. These symptoms can derive from personal factors and/or organizational sources. Therefore, it is helpful to consider what individuals can do to alleviate stress and what organizations can do to facilitate that.

In his excellent video, *Why Zebras Don't Get Ulcers*, Robert Sapolsky notes that being poor and lacking control over your life can make it hard for individuals to manage and cope with stress. However, he notes the importance of having hobbies and connecting with friends and relatives as necessary antidotes. One way to have more control in your life is setting goals and objectives, managing your time and daily schedule effectively, participating in yoga, meditation, sports, and other physical activities, wellness programs, and seeking professional advice and counseling (Sapolsky 2010).

Likewise, organizations have a role to play in minimizing employee stress. They can offer wellness and counseling programs, clarify job roles and expectations in performance reviews, use goal and objective-setting interventions (a persistent recommendation in this book), create a culture that encourages communication and innovation, and ensure in hiring employees that they are well "matched" to their job position.

7

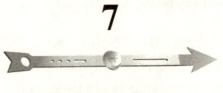

Learning

"Behavior Is a Function of Its Consequences"
—*Skinner*

Perhaps the most valuable and practical theory for leaders (and parents) is to be mindful of B. F. Skinner's "Learning Theory." The key takeaway for practitioners is that "behavior is a function of its consequences." In most organizations, supervisors have a lot of control over the consequences of their subordinates' behaviors. To simplify Skinner, they can reward or punish behavior, and learning to do this effectively is an important skill. In theory, leaders should reward subordinates much more often than resorting to punishment... maybe 10 to 1 as a rule of thumb. Praise, like feedback, should be given in a timely manner, be specific to the act, and can be done in front of others or in private, as the situation warrants. Verbal praise is especially valued. Ken Blanchard wrote a business classic on its importance, *The One Minute Manager* (Blanchard 1971).

Good resources for those interested in knowing more about how to use learning theory effectively are *Analyzing Performance Problems or You Really Oughta Wann* (Mager) or Fred Luthans' superb work on organization behavior modification (OBM) and contingency management.

(See the essay "Positive Psychology and the PSYCAP Model.")

Learning and personality are closely related psychological constructs. As managers, it is important to understand themselves (Aristotle) and to become more self-aware (Goleman). There are several very useful tools to use, such as "Learning Styles" (Kolb), "Myers-Briggs Type Inventory (MBTI)" (Myers-Briggs), and "Career Anchors" (Schein).

Kolb notes that people learn differently and have different preferred styles. To Kolb, the critical domains of learning are "*Concrete Experience* (learning from practice), *Abstract Conceptualization* (learning from theory), *Active Experimentation* (learning by doing), and *Reflective Observation* (learning by contemplating)." Using an inventory to assess styles or preferences, managers can seek to understand better how they prefer to learn, where they might be weak and able to improve, and realize how this affects their influence on others (Kolb 2007).

Myers-Briggs developed an instrument, the MBTI, to also shed light on the elements of one's personality. In their popular model, the key determinants of personality are "*Extroverted* (E)/*Introverted* (I), *Sensors* (S)/*Intuitive* (I), *Thinkers* (T)/*Feelers* (F), and *Judgmental* (J)/*Persuasive* (P)." Preferences for these elements lead to personality "types," like ENTJ or ISTJ (Myers-Briggs 1998).

FORESIGHT

Edgar Schein has developed a handy instrument to assess an individual's "Career Anchor," or one's self-concept and the conditions that must exist in their job to achieve career satisfaction and success. Schein has identified eight different career types: "*Technical Functional* (TF), *General Management* (GM), *Autonomy/Independence* (AU), *Security and Stability* (SE), *Entrepreneur/Creativity* (EC), *Service/Dedication to a Cause* (SV), *Pure Challenge* (CH), and *Lifestyle* (LS)." After assessing one's preferences, it may be possible to "match" one's preferences to a career, profession, or occupation to which they are best suited (Schein 2006).

(See the essay "Positive Psychology and the PSYCAP Model.")

ESSAY: "POSITIVE PSYCHOLOGY AND THE PSYCAP MODEL"

Dr. Fred Luthans of the University of Nebraska-Lincoln has made numerous scholarly contributions to the field of Organization Behavior. He authored the first textbook on the subject in the early '70s and pioneered the field of Organization Behavior Modification (OBM). The essence of OBM is the application of Learning Theory (Skinner) to the theoretical and applied fields of management (Skinner 1971).

Recently, Dr. Luthans has been interested in "positive psychology." His thesis is that much of the psych literature has focused on what is wrong or bothers people, like anxiety, stress, and depression. He thinks more attention should be given to what contributes to and defines a healthy, robust, positive outlook on life. He recognizes that human well-being comes from work, family/friends, and health interrelationships. Much of our outlook on life is determined by our genes (heredity), traits (which are pretty fixed by the age of 30), and a factor he calls "psychological capital" (PSYCAP).

In exhaustive and thorough empirical research, Luthans and his associates have discovered the critical factors that define "psychological capital": Hope, Efficacy, Resilience, and Optimism (or HERO). Hope is the expectation of a better tomorrow. Efficacy is the feeling or confidence that you can accomplish a task. Resilience is the ability to get back up after you have been knocked down. And Optimism relates to whether you see "the glass half full or half empty."

According to Luthans, these factors, which can be learned and developed, explain some of the variances that define a positive outlook on life. His team has taken these lessons into the corporate arena and demonstrated a 250% return on investment in PSYCAP (see Luthans, YouTube). In other words, the cost of training in PSYCAP can be recovered, and considerable profit can be derived from enhanced productivity and effectiveness (Luthans 2004, pp. 45–50).

In conclusion, I think it can be said that we live through a period characterized by hostility, aggression, and polarization. This can be seen in our workplaces, communities, politics, and international relations. Perhaps some of the remedy to this lies in becoming more "emotionally intelligent" (see the earlier essay; Goleman), uniting behind worthy and meaningful causes and endeavors, and striving to improve our own "positivity."

Part Two:
GROUP PROCESSES

1

High-Performing Teams

"There's No 'I' in Team"

—*Anonymous*

Increasingly high-performing organizations are using teams in place of individual work. Teams tend to be more efficient in the long run and produce more creative, accurate, and accepted outcomes. Today, many different types of teams exist, like cross-functional, virtual, project management, and temporary ones. In addition, research has shown that teams tend to go through stages such as "*Forming, Storming, Norming, Performing,* and *Adjourning*" (Maples 1988, pp. 17–23).

Research also shows that highly cohesive teams are more effective than teams low on cohesion. There are many ways to build highly cohesive, high-performing teams. Recently, Coach K, the former Duke basketball coach, was asked about the key elements, or pillars, of successful teams. He noted four factors: "everyone is made to feel important; players must take ownership in the team; they must be able to adjust to setbacks; and everyone must have strong feelings for the team and each other."

Peter Vaill, the noted scholar, has written about "world-class" teams. He notes that "Focus, Feeling, and Time" must be present. Teams need to have a laser like *focus* on their objectives and be very clear on what they want to accomplish. They must have strong *feelings*, passion, even, for the team and each other. Lastly, they must commit significant *time* to preparing for and practicing the skills needed to be successful (Vaill 1982, pp. 23–39).

There are many characteristics of high-performing teams, but some significant ones are: "clear objectives, relevant talent, trust in each other, high commitment, communication emphasis, exceptional leadership, internal encouragement, and external support (Kirkman, Gibson & Shapiro, 2001, pp. 12–29).

Clear Objectives—successful teams are clear on what they want to achieve . . . a national championship, significant business award, or record profitability.

Relevant Talent—it's important to select team members carefully and ensure they are "matched" to their positions/roles. They must also be trainable.

Trust in Each Other—it's important to fully trust other members of the team. Trust is built over time and with experience. It can be difficult and slow to build but quickly broken. Military units need "extreme trust."

High Commitment—setbacks and challenges will always confront teams, but these should be faced, differences resolved, and unity preserved to move forward.

Communication Emphasis—high-performing teams are intentional about information sharing and feedback. Feedback has been called "the breakfast of champions." Communication flows in all directions . . . upward, downward, lateral, and diagonal, and everyone is on the lookout for potential barriers to communication like language differences, distance, power differences, and emotions.

Exceptional Leadership—high-performing teams usually are characterized by strong leaders, coaches, or respected supervisors. They often have high expectations, are good teachers, lead by example, and can articulate a vision and influence others to accomplish it.

Internal Encouragement—usually, effective teams are supported by the larger organization they are a part of. As a result, they can get the resources, funds, and support needed to do the job.

External Support—successful teams are often supported by key people or constituencies outside the organization . . . fans, donors, angel investors, or other key stakeholders.

(See the essay "Teamwork and Synchronization: The 'Blitzkrieg' of the '80s.")

ESSAY:
"TEAMWORK AND SYNCHRONIZATION: THE 'BLITZKRIEG' OF THE '80S"

(Source: initially published in *ARMOR* magazine, July–August 1987)

> "The goal of TACTICS is to create TEAMWORK that reduces the effects of fear on the battlefield"
> —*Ardant du Picq*

In World War II, the German Army developed and employed one of the most potent tactical operational concepts ever seen—the blitzkrieg. Blitzkrieg tactics were characterized by the rapid concentration of forces at a single point, a penetration of enemy defenses, and then a swift and deep exploitation into the enemy's rear, employing all means of maneuver and firepower. It was an extremely effective tactic under World War II battlefield conditions and almost contributed to an Axis victory in the war.

An equally powerful operational concept is being developed today—synchronization, a vital ingredient of AirLand Battle doctrine. Today's battlefield is characterized by tremendous speed, weapons lethality, and complexity. The AirLand Battle doctrine which calls for an offensive spirit and maneuver, fighting a deep, close, and rear battle, and coordination of effort at all tactical levels, and between all services, particularly the army and the air force. AirLand Battle tenets are defined as "agility, initiative, depth, and synchronization."

High-Performing Teams

Synchronization might be described as the ability to integrate all means of combat power and direct it toward a clear purpose. In order to have effective synchronization on the battlefield, there must be effective fighting teams. Synchronization is a by-product of teamwork, and leaders build and lead teams. The key to combat effectiveness is the ability to synchronize all the components of the combined arms. The key to synchronization is the ability to develop teamwork within a unit. How to do that and what the payoffs are is the subject of this article.

Characteristics of Effective Teams

In an excellent paper titled "Building a Winner—On Practice Field and Training Field," Captain Richard Priehm and Mr. Jim Myers (Dallas Cowboys) identified some of the elements of teamwork:

- *Clear Goals.* Someone once said, "if you don't know where you're going, any road will get you there." All units need to have direction and focus. A rotation to the National Training Center (NTC) at Ft. Irwin can provide a common goal for everyone to aim toward.

- *Pick Winners and Stick With 'Em.* In his article, "Leadership: Tapping the Sources of Power," LTG (ret) John F. Forrest writes that the secret of Charlemagne's success in running his empire was the existence of "paladins." These were 12 special knights who had been personally selected and trained to create order out of disorder. Therefore, commanders need to choose winners, clarify responsibilities and expectations, build "habitual relationships" with key staff personnel (i.e., the engineer platoon leader, fire support officer, chaplain, etc.), and work and train all of them as a team. Then they need to support them.

- *Set and Maintain High Standards.* The Dallas Cowboys expect discipline in summer training. They fine players who don't follow the rules. Commanders need to evaluate soldiers on their' individual performance on the SQT and set high standards for such things as preparation of fighting positions, range cards, and personal/vehicle camouflage.

- *Emphasize Physical Conditioning.* Some Task Forces at the NTC "run out of steam" in conducting ground operations. Sometimes it's due to temperatures over 100 degrees and high levels of MOPP. Sometimes it's due to poor physical conditioning. Soldiers in combat need to be alert, aggressive, and self-confident. They develop fit bodies through diet and regular exercise. They build esprit de corps and confidence through "spirit training" (i.e., hand-to-hand drills, bayonet, and pugil stick training) and from challenging leadership courses like the obstacle, confidence, and leaders' reaction courses.

- *Talk and Act Like Winners.* The walls of the West Point gym are filled with sayings like "when the going gets tough, the tough get going" to help motivate cadets. Some coaches like Tom Landry portray a confident "leader image." In addition to confidence, there's a place for humor in commanders' personalities. Humor helps reduce tension in stressful situations and limit battle fatigue's negative consequences. In their classic book, *In Search of Excellence,* Peters and Waterman described some additional characteristics of effective teams like the following:

- *Stick to the Knitting.* Tough, realistic training develops soldiers who are confident and competent. Units going to the NTC emphasize drills, PMCS, MILES proficiency, and always land navigation techniques. Units need opportunities and resources, like money and time, to conduct situational training exercises (STX), ARTEPs, CALFEXs, and gunnery.

- *They Communicate.* According to BG Gordon R. Sullivan, "the ability to effectively process information is, and always has been, the key ingredient of effective fighting units." Commanders need to communicate well—up, down, and laterally. Good units are marked by lots of informal, candid information exchanges. One army Tactical Operations Center (TOC) uses a whistle to assemble key personnel when critical information needs to be disseminated immediately.

- *Power from Rank and File.* All soldiers need to feel like winners. They need to be treated with dignity and respect—from cadet/private to general. Effective units are constantly seeking ways to reward their good soldiers. In turn, superiors get loyalty and respect. It's an exchange process, and subordinates have a crucial role in leadership by helping leaders succeed.

- *Breed Champions.* Commanders need to encourage innovation and let their subordinates experiment. There is no success without failure, and subordinates need the freedom to learn and the freedom to fail.

- *Like Action.* Successful teams are "action-oriented." They like to go out and try things, but they don't try to fix what's not broken.

- *Live by the Spirit and Letter of Belief.* The army values tradition. As Tevye says in *Fiddler on the Roof,* "tradition gives continuity and meaning to life." Good units know what things are important and do them regularly. Commanders need to get out of the office to ensure that important activities are, in fact, going on. That's called "MBWA," management by walking around. Another author who has emphasized the importance of teamwork is Peter Vaill. In his article "The Purposing of High Performing- Systems" Vaill identifies these elements of teams:

— *Social Activities and Operations Are Combined.* In these units, "talking shop" is OK away from the unit. Soldiers like to do things together for the pleasure of each other's company. Informal sessions spring up. People take time to recognize new team members, bid farewell to "old-timers," and thereby humanize an environment marked by great personnel turbulence.

— *Time Is Measured by Key Events.* In these units, people don't talk about "next month"; instead, they speak in terms of "after the ARTEP or STX." Duties are not viewed as something going on between 8:00 a.m. and 5:00 p.m. It's a 24-hour-a-day profession.

— *An "US" Attitude.* There's a genuine commitment to sharing in high-performing teams—not hoarding. Success is measured by how you contribute to making other team members succeed, and the team wins. Competition that creates winners and losers is deemphasized in favor of activities where all win. Statistics aren't used to create a competitive environment between units on "duty" issues. Athletic team competition, however, has a place.

- *Personal Relationship of Equipment and Men.* It's been said that maintenance in the army got worse when the last horses went off active duty. Cavalrymen used to care about their horses, but it's hard to develop an "attachment" to an M3. Some units let their troops name their tracks/tanks to establish a sense of attachment to inanimate machines.

How to Develop Effective Teams

It's one thing to be aware of some of the characteristics of effective teams and another thing to be able to develop effective teams. Some of the key factors in developing effective teams are carefully selecting individuals with the skills, characteristics, and attributes to lead; employing training events, particularly leader training, to mold units out of individuals; and ensuring that the whole team is involved in the significant activities of the command.

The effective AirLand Battle leader must be an effective team builder. He combines the best attributes of teaching and coaching as a mentor. In their article "Leaders as Mentors," LTG Charles W. Bagnal, Earl C. Pence, and LTC Thomas N. Meriwether write that "mentoring is a 'leadership style' which is characterized by open communications with subordinates, role modeling of appropriate values, the effective use of counseling for subordinate development, and sharing of the leader's frame of reference with subordinate leaders." AirLand Battle leaders need to be capable of sharing a vision with their subordinates and helping that vision take form by creating an environment and establishing a climate of command whereby all team members can contribute.

In a letter to the field on "Mentoring," GEN John A. Wickham Jr., the Chief of Staff, wrote that "mentoring is a key way in which we exercise leadership and strengthen army values. Giving of ourselves by sharing our knowledge and experience is the most important legacy we can leave to those who follow." One way teams can be developed then is by leaders consciously applying a "mentoring style" in their relationships with their subordinates. In addition to the presence of a mentoring leader, teamwork can also be developed through training.

One of the best ways to promote teamwork in a unit is to regularly conduct leader training and officer professional development sessions. Some of the best leader training methods include terrain boards and sand tables, simulation exercises, TEWTS, and coordination exercises.

The highly professional German Army of the '40s made extensive use of terrain boards to develop a technique called *auftragstaktik*. Briefly stated, this referred to a condition that could be developed in a tactical unit whereby subordinates learned to operate in a manner consistent with their superior's intent, even when operational orders can't be conveyed. Through wargaming on boards and sand tables, many of the operational lessons of war can be practiced, simulated, and learned.

High-tech simulation devices greatly enhance the army's ability to replicate the reality of combat operations. Simulations such as First Battle, CAMMS, and ARTBASS can be used, and wargames played that enhance tactical performance, awareness, competence, build teams, and develop teamwork.

Coordination exercises, like the fire (FCX), logistics (LCX), and movement coordination (MCX) exercises described in doctrinal training literature can be an efficient means, at a low cost, to enhance coordination between command and staff fires in a FCX, logistical assets, and resources in an LCX. In addition, various movement techniques and methods in a MCX contribute to an ability to synchronize elements of any nature in fighting on the modern battlefield.

To develop effective teams, leaders should involve the "whole team." Wives and family members are a critical part of that team, and special events can be planned to enhance family members' awareness of the unit and its mission. Pre-deployment briefings are an excellent way to convey information to family members prior to off-post deployments or rotations to major training areas. Besides family members, National Guard, Reserve units, and host-nation "partnerships" (or affiliations) often exist, and these units can contribute to or be a part of the "whole team." For example, active army units that train at the NTC often have the chance to augment their personnel strength by deploying with Guard or Reserve soldiers.

The Payoff of Teamwork

The real payoff of teamwork can best be seen in its effects on unit discipline, morale, and actual warfighting ability. At the National Training Center (NTC) at Ft. Irwin, CA, experienced observer-controllers have noted that the most crucial quality distinguishing task forces which perform exceedingly well from others is "discipline." GEN Cavazos once described discipline as "the ability of a soldier to do what was expected of him—even in the absence of superiors or orders." Discipline in combat is demonstrated in many ways—being awake or alert on security, timeliness in conducting missions,

FORESIGHT

performing operations safely, and responsiveness to orders.

Units that train and fight well often have high morale. Soldiers know that their chain of command cares about them, will listen to their concerns (within the constraints of time), and know that what they contribute to the unit mission is regarded as important.

Last and most important, units that demonstrate high levels of teamwork on and off the battlefield WIN. They can accomplish more in less time and capitalize on their ability to get a synergistic effect from their joint cooperation. Proper integration and coordination (synchronization) of all the elements of the combined arms team creates a condition where the sum is greater than the addition of its individual parts. That means units can fight outnumbered—and WIN.

BIBLIOGRAPHY

Bagnal, GEN Charles W., Pence, Earl C., and LTC Thomas N. Meriwether. "Leaders as Mentors," *Military Review*, July 1985.

Depuy, GEN William E. "Toward Balanced Doctrine." *Army* magazine, November 1984.

Forrest, LTG John F. "Leadership: Tapping the Source of Power." *Army* magazine, January 1984.

FM 100-5, Operations Manual.

Odiorne, George S. "Mentoring An American Management Innovation." Personnel Administrator, May 1985.

Peters, Thomas J., and Robert H. Waterman, Jr. *In Search of Excellence*, Harper and Row Publishers, Inc., 1982.

Priehm, CPT Richard, and Jim Myers. "Building a Winner—On Practice Field and Training Field." Concept paper submitted to US Army Teleconference Net (Delta Force) May 1982.

Vaill, Peter. "The Purposing of High-Performing Systems." Paper prepared for conference on "Administrative Leadership: New Perspectives on Theory and Practice," University of Illinois, 1981.

2

Diversity and Multigenerational Teams

"Diversity is the one true thing we all have in common"
—*Winston Churchill*

Diversity in an organization is how people are different yet similar to one another. People can be different from each other based on many factors, such as race, religion, age, and sexual preference, to name a few.

Many authors have written about the presence of a multigenerational workforce in organizations today. Many typologies exist, but one way to view this generational spread is World War II (pre-1928); the Silent Generation (1928–'45); Baby Boomers (1946–'64); Generation X (1965–'80); Generation Y (1980–2000); Millennials (2000–'10); and Gen Z (2010–present). The generations differ in many characteristics, but among them are dedication and loyalty to jobs and employers, awareness and skill with computer technology, acceptance of authority, preference for individual or group interaction, and overall drive and commitment to work.

World War II and Silent Generations are still present and influential in the workplace, often as CEOs and board members. This generation endured and survived the sacrifices, hardships, and services required by World War II, the Depression, and the Korean War. They emerged from these historical events with attitudes of "lucky to be alive," appreciation for a job, and frugality in their approach to consumption. They were very dedicated, committed, and loyal to their organization. In return, a social, informal contract prevailed, giving them lifetime careers and employment.

The large birth rate created the Baby Boomer generation following the wars of the '40s and '50s. This generation witnessed the social changes of the '60s with challenges to authority, experimentation with unconventional dress, drugs, and social norms, and the start of the Vietnam War and antiwar and civil rights protests. Boomers also saw the collapse of the "job for life" unwritten contract with employers as many of their parents were displaced by advances in automation and technology.

Generation X and Y were significantly influenced by the rapid growth of personal computers and smartphone technologies. Many of them learned these critical job skills in secondary schools and quickly found jobs in all types of organizations. In addition, they were comfortable with working in groups and teams on workplace projects. They too were affected by the loss of a "social contract" with employers.

Millennials and Gen Z employees now constitute the largest number of employees in the workplace. They too are highly skilled in technology and have the ability (and preference) to work remotely. The COVID pandemic has allowed many of this generation to continue working while others were separated from jobs and income. This generation is looking for "meaning" in their jobs and seeking balance in work-life relationships.

Many challenges exist for organizations to effectively confront diversity issues like the "glass ceiling," bias, and stereotyping. To do this, many organizations have developed innovative training, mentoring, and coaching programs. As always, progressive policies, commitment, and involvement from the top are required.

(See the essay "The Sense of a Goose.")

ESSAY:
"THE SENSE OF A GOOSE"

(Source: Unknown)

Next fall, when you see geese heading south for the winter flying along in a "V" formation, you might be interested in knowing what science has discovered about why they fly that way. It has been learned that as each bird flaps its wings, it creates an uplift for the bird immediately following. By flying in a "V" formation, the whole flock adds at least 71% greater flying range than if each bird flew on its own.

Whenever a goose falls out of formation, it suddenly feels the drag and resistance of trying to go it alone and quickly gets back into formation to take advantage of the lifting power of the bird immediately in front. When a lead goose gets tired, it rotates to the back, and another bird takes over. The geese honk from behind to encourage those up front to keep up their speed.

When a goose gets sick or is wounded by gunshots and falls out, two geese fall out of the formation and follow it down to help and protect it. They stay with the bird until it can fly or die, and they then launch out on their own or with another formation to catch up with the group.

This is a story of teamwork and working in harmony; of mutually supporting each other, in good times and bad; of being willing to share leadership and delegate; of actively communicating with each other as objectives are being pursued; and of sacrificing for each other and "leaving no goose behind"

Part Three:
ORGANIZATION DYNAMICS

1

Strategy

"If You Don't Know Where You Are Going, Any Road Will Get You There"

—Anonymous

An important responsibility of senior executive officers and their top teams is to develop effective business plans and strategies for operating a business or any organization. Developing products and services that people are willing to pay for is the essence of corporate leadership.

Strategies are essential to any organization. Some examples of successful strategies include the US Army in planning the invasion of Europe—Operation Overlord (D-Day), Southwest Air CEO Herb Kelleher in stockpiling jet fuel at low prices and weathering big increases in fuel costs that bankrupted other airlines, and Honda in utilizing quality design and management techniques in the '70s to build cars that lasted longer to capture the automobile market.

Several conceptual tools help achieve a competitive advantage over rivals. One of the most elegant is a model called SWOT analysis. SWOT stands for "Strengths, Weaknesses, Opportunities, and Threats." Organizations can conduct an internal analysis of their company's Strengths and Weaknesses, and an external analysis, Opportunities and Threats, to identify potentially valuable insights and courses of action to improve. *Strengths* are things the organization does well. *Weaknesses* are areas in need of improvement. *Opportunities* are potential actions not being done that could be. And *Threats* are the actions of rivals and competitors negatively impacting the organization.

Another critical model related to strategy is the "Open-System Model." All organizations can be viewed as "open-systems" with Inputs, Throughputs, Outputs, a Feedback Loop, and the External Environment (Katz and Kahn 1966, pp. 14–30). This model is discussed in more detail in the essay "Open-Systems: Ignore at Your Peril." Senior executives must constantly be monitoring and interacting with their "external environment" and not be blindsided by changes that impact their organizations. An essay by Barker discusses the interesting concept of "Paradigms" and "Paradigm Shifts."

(See Fig. 1, *"An Open-System Model of Organization"*; essays, "Open-Systems: Ignore at Your Peril"; and "Paradigms.")

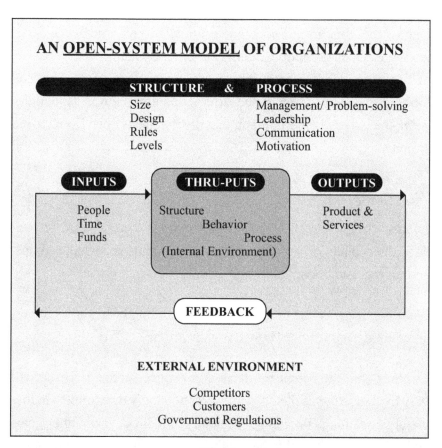

Fig. 1

ESSAY: "OPEN-SYSTEMS: IGNORE AT YOUR PERIL"

One of the most useful conceptual models in organizational studies is the Open-System Model. The Open-System Model consists of five essential elements: inputs, throughputs, outputs, feedback loops, and consideration of the external environment. It is that element, the external environment, that distinguishes open from closed systems.

The Elements:

Inputs—primarily consist of those resources that are used to produce the product or service. Examples of inputs are people, funds, equipment, and, most importantly, time.

Throughputs—are the range of activities and processes used in creating goods and services by the organization.

Outputs—are the actual products and services created. These will vary by the nature of the organization but greatly determine whether the organization is operating efficiently and effectively. Other goals and objectives are established with these desired outcomes in mind.

Feedback Loops—to improve, all organizations (and people) require timely, specific, and accurate feedback on whether desired standards are being met. To improve the quality of their product or service, many organizations currently rely on surveys and questionnaires to gauge customer satisfaction.

External Environment—in my mind, this is THE most crucial factor to consider in the Open-System Model. There are general and specific factors to consider in the environment. Some of these are competitors, government regulations, customers, unions, and social, economic, political, and demographic factors.

The Open-System Model is a very useful way to think about ANY organization. It causes key leaders and decision-makers to focus on all the key elements that most contribute to an organization's effectiveness. Failing to attend to critical dynamics and changes occurring in the external environment has often resulted in the decline and demise of an enterprise. (Katz & Kahn 1966, pp. 14–30).

ESSAY: "PARADIGMS"

One concept in the organizational literature that has taken on a "larger-than-life" meaning is that of "paradigms." The term was initially popularized by Joel Barker, the writer, trainer, and OD practitioner, years ago (Barker 1989, video).

A "paradigm" is a pattern, model, or "way of looking" at a subject. In business, it is not uncommon to have "paradigm shifts" when a significant change results in new ways of looking at things. In my view, the shift is often triggered by revolutionary technological changes. If organizations don't monitor change occurring in their external environment, they will often find themselves out of luck . . . and business. Following are some interesting examples:

During the American Civil War, the army was slow to adjust its tactical doctrine (how units are meant to fight) to significant improvements in weaponry, particularly rifle bullet accuracy. The result was a bloody, lethal war.

In camera technology, Kodak was slow to adjust to the technology of digital cameras. Polaroid was around, but profits from film and processing were hard to sacrifice. Bankruptcy loomed.

In watch technology, nobody did gears and mechanisms better than the Swiss. But they were slow to adapt to digital technology, and the appeal of numbers over minute/second hands and symbols has prevailed. (As an aside, if there's a teen in your house, check and see if they can read a nondigital clock or watch. From my limited sample experiment over the years, odds are . . . they can't.)

The concept of "paradigms" is interesting and worthy of continued reflection and analysis.

2

Organization Culture

"Message to CEOs: Culture Begins With You"
—Anonymous

Organization Culture can be viewed as the values, principles, traditions, and, in short, the "ways of doing things" within an organization. A related concept is Organization Climate, which is about "how things feel" in an organization. Cultures can be strong or weak depending on how widely shared beliefs are held. In recent years, organization leaders have become very intentional about creating cultures that emphasize ethics, innovation, quality, customers, and even spirituality by recognizing the innate goodness and potential of their employees, partners, and other stakeholders.

Socialization can be viewed as how employees learn about their unique culture. High-performing organizations pay particular attention to this by holding meaningful "onboarding" programs for new members that might include presentations and interactions with senior leaders, information on the company's history and mission, values, vision, and core principles. Sometimes these orientations can go on for several days and include tours of campuses and facilities.

Culture comes from many unique sources but often includes stories of founders, rituals, symbols, and even unique language or jargon. No two organizations' cultures are the same.

Stories can strengthen culture and often relate to founders, milestones, and memorable events. For example, part of the unique culture of the US Military Academy at West Point is shaped and reinforced by historic graduates depicted in granite monuments around the grounds, like Washington, Jefferson, Grant, Eisenhower, Patton, and the American Soldier. In addition, many business stories are told about charismatic legends like Kroc, Knight, Iacocca, Welch, Jobs, and Gates. These stories, often with life lessons, help bring organizations to life.

Rituals can also be a potential source of cultural enrichment. For instance, colleges have Investiture, Baccalaureate, and Graduation ceremonies. Businesses can hold awards and holiday parties. And the military prides itself on promotion ceremonies, monthly hails and farewells, and change of command events.

Sometimes culture reveals itself in the form of *symbols*. In the military, flags are powerful symbols even displayed on caskets. In academia, the mace has special meaning at ceremonies, and in churches, ancient scrolls, fonts, and even sculptures convey special meaning and significance.

Lastly, *language* can be an element of organization culture. Many unique and distinctive acronyms are often used. The military, government, and corporations are filled with colorful jargon that has unique meaning and interpretation to insiders.

Research indicates that organizational culture can be "managed." One way in which this is done is by who is selected and hired for membership. Organizations often hire people they feel will fit in and adapt well to the culture. In a parallel manner, people are also "deselected" (or fired) because of a lack of a good "match" with the culture. Hopefully, this only occurs after performance counseling, training, and attempts at development.

3

Organization Development/ Effectiveness (OD/OE)

"Tradition provides continuity and meaning to life"
—Tevye, *Fiddler on the Roof)*

At its core, Organization Development/Effectiveness uses a four-step model similar to a "Doctor-Patient" process. That is, *"Diagnosis, Action-Planning, Intervention,* and *Evaluation."* In the diagnosis step, consultants often use surveys, observations, and interviews to collect data about a problem. Next, action -planning is done to carefully analyze and interpret initial data and findings and weigh other potentially relevant information. In the intervention phase, proven, tested, and reliable programs and strategies are often pursued to improve outcomes. Finally, an evaluation must be done to ensure that the chosen intervention has been successful and that no further actions or adjustments are required (Schein 1969, pp. 6–7).

The OD/OE strategy most often used is "Survey Feedback." In this instance, insights or data derived from the initial diagnosis is "fed back" to organization leaders and stakeholders. This often results in increased awareness and responses which can lead to self-evident and effective results.

Other OD/OE strategies include, but are not limited to, LEAN programs to eliminate or reduce waste in processing; Six-Sigma programs to reduce or eliminate errors; Total Quality Management (TQM) initiatives to improve product (or service) quality; Process Improvement strategies to improve basic processes like communication, planning, decision-making, leadership, conflict resolution, diversity, and team building to improve small-group functioning, morale, and effectiveness.

I believe Organization Development/Effectiveness may be the most important and relevant area for would-be leaders, practitioners, and entrepreneurs to understand, appreciate, and master. The pace of change in today's institutional "external environment" is without precedent, and it behooves all players to commit to adaptability, continuous improvement, and innovation. The concepts, theories, and models found in the OD/OE literature can help and are a major theme of this book.

(See the essays "Organization Dynamics in the Future" and "Organization Change and Development".) There is some repetition in text here to reinforce key concepts.

ESSAY: "ORGANIZATION DYNAMICS IN THE FUTURE"

As a young graduate student in the '70s, I had the opportunity to take a seminar taught by the dean of the business school, George Odiorne. At the time, he was regarded as one of America's pre-eminent management scholar-practitioners and a "management by objectives" guru. Moreover, he was a protégé of Peter Drucker. In class one day, I asked him why studying the future was so important. His classic reply was, "because that's where we will spend the rest of our lives." So, what might that future hold in store regarding issues like organizational design, leadership imperatives, and the role of "followers" in the future paradigm of organizational life? What follows are some brief reflections on these.

Organizational design in the future is likely to be heavily influenced by key dependent variables from the past, efficiency, and effectiveness. Predictably, for-profit and not-for-profit organizations will likely become flatter (i.e., fewer hierarchical levels), more decentralized, organic, and leaner. There will continue to be a significant emphasis on quality, reducing errors, eliminating waste, sustainability, and self-sufficiency. Employees will seek out companies with a reputation for creating cultures where people can grow and develop (not shrink) and are socially responsible. Frederick Herzberg, the noted motivation theorist on the faculty with Odiorne, said it will be "efficient for organizations to be human." That is to say that organizations will need to treat employees with dignity and respect and compensate employees as generously as they can for their critical contribution to the "bottom line."

Those who aspire to lead in future organizations will, more than ever, need to possess a "service-oriented" leadership style. Their role will be to inspire, provide a vision, and serve their customers, stakeholders, and employees to their utmost ability.

In addition, leaders will need knowledge and skills related to diagnosing situations and being adaptable, flexible, and agile in implementing strategies and solutions, evaluating their effectiveness, and adjusting as required. This competence will derive from their inherent personality characteristics, more androgynous than traditionally male or female, and experience, training, and awareness of current theories, concepts, and models from the social, behavioral, and administrative sciences. Finally, successful managers and leaders of tomorrow will need to be well skilled in what Daniel Goleman called "emotional intelligence." Underlying his construct is the notion that EQ (self-awareness, self-regulation, empathy, motivation, and social skills), not just IQ, are the keys to effective leadership (Goleman 1998).

Lastly, here are some thoughts on "followers" in future organizations. The term "follower" (found in empirical leadership research) may be outdated as employees will be viewed more as colleagues, associates, partners, and stakeholders. Mary Parker Follett was one of the few organization theorists to focus on the critical role played by "followers" in organization settings and leadership. According to her research, "followers" are crucial because if they dislike or disapprove of their leader, they could restrict effort to the task at hand or withhold essential, mission-related information that could negatively impact task success (Follett 1941). One interesting area of study from sociology that relates to this phenomenon is the power of "lower participants" in organizations. "Followers" are indeed "people" too, and future leaders and organizations will need to provide not only a job but a *good* job that includes an investment in training and development.

In this brief essay, I have tried to identify some emerging patterns associated with future organizational life. These insights should be considered in planning for, designing, and leading effective organizations in the future.

ESSAY: "ORGANIZATION CHANGE AND DEVELOPMENT"

"Things that don't change remain the same"
—*Anonymous*

Organization Development (OD) refers to a field of study (theory) and consulting strategies (practice) to improve organizational effectiveness and manage organizational change. It involves using knowledge from the administrative, social, and behavioral sciences to design structures and processes to respond better to changes in an organization's internal and external environments. This article will address a helpful framework for analyzing change (the open-systems model), describe the four-step OD model, and identify some of the OD interventions in use today. Two particularly useful OD interventions, *Management by Objectives* and *Job Enrichment*, will be discussed in detail.

The Open-Systems Model is an excellent place to start in analyzing OD. The model consists of five elements—input, throughput, output, a feedback loop, and the external environment. Organizational inputs include raw materials, people, capital, and information. Time can also be considered a critical organizational input. These inputs are then transformed through a series of activities—employees direct and create, employers mold and guide, and technology and operations convert raw materials into outputs. In general, outputs are the products and services created that a customer is willing to pay for. Feedback refers to the information and data about how well the product was received and how efficiently the product was produced. This information can improve the product or service over time and respond to changes in the internal environment. The last element is the external environment. This may be the most crucial element of the model. Effective organizations must consistently monitor what is going on in the external environment and be prepared to adapt and react to changing circumstances.

Organization theory literature is filled with tragic case studies of organizations that failed to do this- the armed forces, the US auto companies in the '70s, etc. Customers, unions, suppliers, distributors, and local, state, and federal government agencies are located in the external environment. An important strategic function for top management is continuously engaging with these groups and monitoring societal trends and forecasts that impact the organization.

(Katz & Kahn, 1966)

The OD "Four-Step Model" is an effective way to conceptualize what OD is all about. The four steps of the model are- diagnosis, action- plan, intervention, and evaluation. Consultants often use observation, interviews, instruments, or surveys when diagnosing organizations. These tools enable consultants to determine where the organization is today. After data is collected, the next step is action- planning, where other sources of information are reviewed about the organization, and some initial planning and potential courses of action are formulated. Next is intervention, where some strategy or program is implemented to address issues, problems, or opportunities identified in earlier steps. These potential interventions, like survey feedback, Lean Manufacturing, Six Sigma, etc., will be addressed later. Lastly, and most importantly, comes the evaluation step. This step is critical to determining how well the intervention has worked . . . or not. Did it help to resolve problems or issues or make the organization more effective? So, not unlike a "Doctor-Patient" process, specimens have been collected, information shared, medications or procedures prescribed, and a follow-up check has been completed (Schein 1969).

Reference was made to possible OD interventions, which will be briefly reviewed here. These are some of the most used OD interventions.

- a. *Survey Feedback.* This is probably the most common OD intervention. In this case, surveys collect data on where employees and the organization are today. For example, surveys can assess employee morale, organizational culture, or job satisfaction. After collecting and processing, this information or the results are fed to interested parties, usually in training or coaching sessions.
- b. *Lean Manufacturing.* This OD intervention focuses on reducing or eliminating waste in the organization. How can manufacturing by-products that have value be captured and potentially capitalized on? In practice, a lean program can create a "waste inspector," whose job is to identify waste sources, perhaps excess use of paper and copying in the workplace, and take intentional action to limit supply and reproduction to reduce expenses.
- c. *Six Sigma.* The goal of Six Sigma is to reduce errors in the manufacturing process. Using a process of "Defining, Measuring, Analyzing, Improving, and Controlling," the goal is to reduce defects to a desired level of 3.4 defects

per million opportunities or trials. Quality tools that are used include Control Charts, Process Mapping, Root Cause Analysis, Tree Diagrams, and Statistical Process Control. This intervention has been used effectively in manufacturing/assembly line settings and hospitals.

Other OD interventions include team building, sensitivity training, and Total Quality Management. Each of these programs has unique methods and tools designed to target and improve organizational effectiveness in some intentional way.

In this essay, I would like to focus on two OD interventions that prior research and practice indicate they have particular merit if implemented well. These are Management by Objectives and Job Enrichment.

Management by Objectives (MBO) is an OD intervention first pioneered by Dr. George Odiorne, the "father of MBO." Odiorne was a student of Peter Drucker, and he had a distinguished career in business and academia. Studies from psychology and the administrative sciences clearly document the importance and power of goals and objectives to superior individual and organizational performance. Odiorne and his disciples got interested in setting objectives and goals when they collected data from organizations. For example, the team would ask supervisors what their team members were working on and record the responses. Then they would ask employees what they were doing and found a big disconnect. The consultants concluded that this contributed to a lack of efficiency and effectiveness. Out of this, MBO was born.

Odiorne defined MBO as "a process whereby the superior and

subordinate managers of an organization jointly identify its common objectives, define each individual's major areas of responsibility in terms of the results expected, and use these measures as guides for operating the unit and assessing the contribution of each of its members" (Odiorne 1965).

The MBO process itself consists of four steps. In Step 1, the supervisor shares their objectives and emphasizes key priorities for the unit. In Step 2, the associate shares their objectives for the upcoming quarter or period. In Step 3, there is quarterly, face-to-face performance feedback and counseling. Step 4 is the audit or evaluation step, which is often conducted annually. Ideally, this step will include preparation by the associate of a Support Form where they can note not only their objectives but also their assessment in writing of how well their objectives were achieved... or not. Key to the whole process is a focus on objectives (or desired end results), periodic feedback and communication between parties, and then a final evaluation that includes input from employees. This strategy can enhance organizational efficiency and effectiveness and be performed in a collegial, intentional, and committed way (Odiorne 1965).

In MBO, the focus is on individual objectives, but it can be helpful to have broader organizational goals. The primary focus of MBO is for each individual, top to bottom in the organization, to have current performance objectives. Odiorne envisioned four types of objectives: Routine, Problem-Solving, Innovative, and Personal Development. Ideally, all organization members would have one or two objectives of each type. Routine objectives reflect the core duties or responsibilities of a job. Successful completion of these ensures continued employment. Problem-solving objectives are focused on fixing an existing problem at the workplace. These can be recent problems or long-standing ones. It can be helpful to use Dewey's classic problem-solving model in designing these objectives: Define the problem, Collect data/information, Develop courses of action or alternative solutions, Implement or Execute, and finally, Evaluate. The third type of objective is innovation. An innovative objective does not need to be original and new, like a PhD dissertation, but something new to the job or organization. Lastly, Personal Development objectives are included. Examples of this objective might be physical fitness goals, attending workshops, courses, and seminars to grow intellectually, or even planning to expand one's family (Odiorne 1965).

In developing objectives in support of MBO, all organization members should have a basic knowledge of setting objectives. The SMART acronym is helpful in this regard. Objectives should be Specific, Measurable, Attainable, and Realistic and include milestones or Time intervals. An objective setting is a fluid, dynamic process, not fixed in concrete. They are best set in pencil with lots of erasing and revising over time as feedback is provided, conditions change, and results are achieved. Putting objectives on laminated cards, always ready for inspection, runs counter to the spirit and adaptability of MBO and leads to rigidity and failure.

There are several keys to success in the implementation of an MBO program. The first is "start at the top." Ideally, CEOs would understand MBO and have personal objectives. It is possible, however, to "pilot" an MBO system in a department or subset of the company. Second, as previously noted, all subunits of the organization should be involved as much as possible. Third, consideration should be given to using an external consultant—or not—to establish the program. There are many pros and cons to involving outside parties in the process, but it is essential to have a basic level of competence and knowledge related to MBO. Fourth, it is vital to allow time for MBO to take root. Initial training is required, potential resistance must be overcome, best practices need to be developed, and expertise must be acquired. At its core, MBO is essentially good management practice. Lastly, as noted earlier, the "boilerplate" is to be avoided (Odiorne 1965).

Job Enrichment is another OD intervention pioneered by Fred Herzberg, the "father of Job Enrichment." Dr. Herzberg was the author of many books on worker satisfaction and motivation, but his classic book is *Work and the Nature of Man.* He was a distinguished academician, international consultant, and prolific writer. His most significant articles were published in the *Harvard Business Review*, "One More Time: How Do You Motivate Employees?" and "The Wise Old Turk." In addition, his Motivation-Hygiene theory is published in all management-related texts.

Using the "critical incident" research methodology, Herzberg concluded that there were different factors involved in worker satisfaction (the motivators) and worker dissatisfaction (the hygiene factors). Specifically, Herzberg found that employees at all levels were motivated by achievement, recognition, the work itself (importantly), advancement, and growth. On the other hand, employees were dissatisfied with the hygiene factors- supervision, company policy, relationships with supervisors, working conditions, salary (interestingly), relationships with peers, personal life, relationships with subordinates, status, and security. Therefore, awareness and understanding of these factors were critical for effectively managing and motivating people in organizations of any type.

Herzberg's Job Enrichment strategy, or intervention, focuses on "building the motivator factors into individual/personal job descriptions." The essential ingredients of an enriched job are the following:

a. *Meaning*—all jobs should be meaningful. To Herzberg, everyone's work was important, almost sacred, with significant implications for the individual's psychological and physical health and the organization's.

b. *A Client Function*—everyone in an organization, even assembly line workers, should know the stakeholders, clients, and customers who buy and benefit from the company's products and services.

c. *A Growth Function*—all organizations should grow their employees through investments in training, technology, and self-development.

d. *Opportunity to Schedule Own Work*—as much as possible, employees should be able to pace and structure their work activities and objectives as they see best.

e. *Skill Variety, Identity, and Significance*—workers should be challenged with new work opportunities (job rotation) and not be assigned repetitive, boring tasks with no variability over time.

f. *Autonomy*—workers should be able to schedule their own work and have the freedom to pursue it without constant monitoring, controlling, and oversupervision (micromanagement).

g. *Feedback*—this ingredient has been called "the breakfast of champions." All workers need specific, timely feedback on how they are doing and how they can improve. This is most important for young or inexperienced workers. Feedback needs to be planned, intentional, and with more positive than negative messages (Herzberg 1966).

h. *Other Factors*—like company culture, climate, philosophy, and reinforcement of "servant leadership" principles should be encouraged throughout the organization.

4

Organization Conflict and Innovation

"All Conflict Is Not Bad, and Innovation Is Job One"
—*Anonymous*

Organization leaders today need skills in managing conflict and need to know how to stimulate innovation.

The first thing to note about conflict is that it's not all bad. Conflict can sometimes indicate healthy disagreement on organization projects and policies, competition between individuals and subunits, and concern and passion for the organization. Too little or no conflict can be a sign of apathy and disengagement. On the other hand, too much conflict can result in dysfunction, sabotage, and failure to meet objectives.

Pondy has developed a helpful model for both analyzing and managing conflict (Pondy 1967, pp. 296–320). His model has five stages of conflict: Latent, Perceived, Felt, Manifest, and Aftermath. In the

Latent stage, no conflict exists, but there is a high potential for it due to competition for resources, differing objectives, bureaucratic factors, or a "win-lose" mentality. In the *Perceived* stage, people are aware of the conflict, and escalation of positions occurs. In the *Felt* stage, people begin to polarize, and further escalation ensues. In the *Manifest* stage, fighting and aggression are underway, and the organization experiences negative effects on efficiency and effectiveness. Finally, the *Aftermath* is characterized by the resolution of the conflict and/or efforts by parties to heal the damage inflicted. Leaders and managers should be aware of these stages, analyze the situation they confront, and develop effective strategies to intervene and limit the damage of the conflict or resolve it early in the process. Potential strategies could be structural or process changes to the organization or perhaps some form of awareness and sensitivity training to change attitudes and behavior.

Many successful CEOs, like Jack Welch (GE) and Elon Musk (Tesla), believe that innovation is the most crucial process in organizations. Innovation can either be "revolutionary" or "incremental," depending on how quickly its effects are felt. For example, in the military, weapons innovation can trigger rapid effects on warfighting doctrine (revolutionary), whereas changes in computer technology tend to be more incremental.

Modern leaders have many tools at their disposal to manage innovation. Among these are experimenting with project management, cross-functional teams, skunk works, new venture divisions, and encouraging through culture piloting and experimentation.

(See the essay "Innovation—The Nuthatch Way.")

ESSAY: "INNOVATION—THE NUTHATCH WAY"

One of the nice things about living on Long Island is observing migrating birds in the fall and spring. Each year, I see a wide variety of birds hiding in our bushes, nesting in our trees, pecking at our feeders, and drinking from our birdbaths. It's fun to watch! Over the years, I've seen countless doves, blue jays, robins, sparrows, and grackles, along with crows, woodpeckers, juncos, hawks, seagulls (we're near the water), and, one of my favorites... **NUTHATCHES.**

Nuthatches are not too special to look at. They are small, gray, and white, but they are really different in one respect. Most birds search for food and parasites as they go *UP* trees. However, nuthatches follow "the road not taken" by searching cracks and crevices while going *DOWN* trees. You have probably seen them doing their thing in your yard.

To me, nuthatches and their unusual habit might be illustrative of people we know who "think outside the box," do things a little differently, and who we probably admire for their independence, creativity, and, perhaps, boldness.

I don't know if nuthatches have an easier go of it in their world than others of their species, but I do know they're benefiting from the habit of "marching to a different drum"—looking down and discovering a banquet for themselves that others who are headed up have missed along the way.

5

Ethics and Social Responsibility

*"Ignore Ethics at Your Peril and Begin with
No Lying, Cheating, or Stealing"*
—*Anonymous*

One way of looking at the complex subject of ethics is as principles about right and wrong behavior and practices. Exploring morals gets us into the issues of "good and bad." There are different approaches to ethics, like *utilitarian* (the greatest good for the greatest number) and *social justice* and *rights* perspectives. One can take an "absolute" approach toward ethics, exemplified by codes and commandments with no exceptions, or a "situational" approach, where "it depends on the situation" how one should act in a given circumstance.

The essay "Professional Ethics—Briefly Noted" discusses a very pragmatic view of ethics. What *causes* people to act unethically, and what can individuals and organizations *do* about that? The sure way for unethical behavior to triumph is for people in positions of responsibility to ignore the subject or do nothing about it.

A related concept to ethics is that of social responsibility. There are two schools of thought on this: the "classical" view (Milton Friedman) that proposes that the fundamental task of business organizations is to make money and be profitable, and the "socioeconomic" view that calls for protecting and improving society, a macro perspective (Friedman 1962, p. 126).

Archie Carroll and others have proposed a useful model or "pyramid" way of looking at social responsibility. Organizations and their leaders should be cognizant of "economic, legal, ethical, and philanthropic (or discretionary)" factors and consider all these in making decisions and operating companies. Unfortunately, examples abound of companies making extraordinary profits in *legal* ways but conveniently failing to consider what was *ethical and the right thing to do*. The case of cigarette manufacturers in the last century comes to mind, and millions of consumers' health were negatively impacted when the harmful effects were widely known (Carroll 1991, p. 42).

There are many great resources, books, and films available to those wanting to raise their ethical and social awareness levels, books like the *Bible*, the *Best and Brightest*, and *A Bright Shining Lie*, and films like *A Man for All Seasons, Gandhi, Devil's Advocate,* and *To Kill a Mockingbird*.

There are many reasons why leaders today should aspire to be socially responsible. First, more consumers consider social responsibility reputations when investing their personal resources. Also, many significant polls and inventories rank companies on their corporate social responsibility (CSR) programs and policies. And finally, because it's now considered the "right thing to do" and companies' "bottom lines" are being rewarded. Perhaps Fred Herzberg put it best when he noted, "it's efficient to be human."

(See the essay "Professional Ethics—Briefly Noted.")

ESSAY: "PROFESSIONAL ETHICS— BRIEFLY NOTED"

Not too many years ago, a prominent business leader in New York City noted that "educating and training people on the subject of ethics was not worth the effort because it couldn't be done." Indeed, in business and other professional schools across the country in the 20th century, it would have been hard to find a core course in ethics or the topic even addressed in an academic curriculum. Ethics and corporate social responsibility have recently become "hot topics" in academia, professional training, and education. But evidence abounds of ethical "meltdowns" and misconduct in all types of organizations—banks (Royal Bank of Scotland), corporations (ENRON), government (George Washington Bridge scandal), public school systems (changing student test scores), etc. This brief essay will address ethics, what causes people to act unethically, and what should be done to prevent it.

Ethics relates to principles, standards, and values that guide honorable behavior. It is distinguishing "right from wrong" and then doing the right thing. Scholars have viewed ethics from many perspectives. Absolute ethics calls for people to adhere to strict codes or commandments. Situational ethics notes that one should consider the influence of external factors in determining "right from wrong." In his "stages of moral development," Robert Kohlberg offers even more insight into the nature of moral and ethical decision-making. He has written elegantly about the moral stages individuals progress through from infancy to adulthood.

FORESIGHT

What causes people to act unethically in group settings? It is a complex, multifaceted issue, but some of the usual culprits are: greed, dishonesty, lack of time or resources, conflicting guidance, ambition, excessive "bottom-line" emphasis, and the organizational paradigm of "producing more with less" (no matter what the collateral damage). In my experience, some of the worst ethical lapses have occurred when tremendous pressure is put on young supervisors who are often overworked and under resourced to just "make it happen" and get results.

What can organizations do about this? Fortunately, many programs and strategies can be pursued. Among these are the following: personal example of senior leaders (never underestimate this), developing an internal code of ethics, training supervisors and employees in topics related to fraud, waste, and abuse, rewarding people who report ethical lapses, instituting negative consequences for potential "bad actors," unannounced audits, and involving fiduciaries more in oversight. Many of these steps only require emphasis and can be instituted without significant cost to the organization. However, failing to act proactively or hoping that issues will "just go away" or might "never surface" can be very costly. It can also greatly damage the organization's hard-earned reputation.

TRAINING is one of the most effective strategies for promoting an ethical culture. Workshops can be designed to allow senior leaders to address ethics. Short cases can be developed using business scenarios and examples, allowing time for group analysis and discussion. The value is in learning from different perspectives and exploring diverse views. In this manner, organizations can proactively diffuse potential issues before they occur.

People run organizations, and people are capable of lapses in moral judgment and acting out of unethical self-interest. Therefore, it behooves all organizations in the 21st century to attend to the issue of ethics through policy, example, and training, just as they would other "bottom-line" challenges. Research suggests that ethical awareness and sensitivity can indeed be taught. Moral courage may then be called for to do the right thing and pursue the harder right over the easier wrong.

6

Organization Design

Axiom #1, "Structure Conditions and Controls Behavior"
—*Carvalho*

To be effective in the 21st century, leaders and managers need to be aware of and skilled at organizational design. In many ways, they are architects of their organizations. In design, organizations must be "matched" to the environments where they operate. In fast-moving and changing environments, which most organizations are in today, they need to be agile and adaptable, and structures and processes need to be "tailored" to be effective. For example, the US Army "tailors" units to different tactical environments by creating an organization chart so that the structure "matches" the situation. On the other hand, structures and processes can be slower to change and more stable in slow, static, bureaucratic environments.

One helpful concept or construct related to this is the "Four Challenges of Organization Design" (Jones 2013, pp. 92–121). Relevant factors of this model are "*Differentiation* (or specialization) to *Integration* (or coordination*)*; *Centralization* to *Decentralization* (or decision-making from high to low); *Standardization* (rules and procedures) to *Mutual Adjustment* (flexibility in execution); and *Mechanistic* to *Organic* design." Executives can apply the above constructs to analyze and design their companies to be more efficient and effective by "matching" their design to the environment they operate in.

Organizations can be designed in traditional ways, by function or division, or in modern, contemporary ways, like teams, matrixes, networks, or virtual designs. Each has unique advantages and disadvantages that must be carefully weighed and considered to achieve strategic goals and objectives.

References

Barker, J. (1989). "The Business of Paradigms" (VHS/DVD).

Blanchard, K. & R. Conley. (2022). *Simple Truths of Leadership*, Polvera Publishing.

Carroll, A. B. (1991). "The Pyramid of Corporate Social Responsibility: Toward the Moral Management of Organizational Stakeholders," *Business Horizons*, Jul–Aug.

Cohen, M. D., March, J. G. & J. P. Olsen. (1972). "A Garbage Can Model of Organizational Choice," *Administrative Science Quarterly*.

Facella, P. (with A. Genn). (2009). *Everything I Know About Business I Learned At McDonald's*, McGraw-Hill, NY.

Follett, M. P. *Freedom and Coordination*. (1933). Management Publications Trust, London.

Friedman, M. (1962). "The Social Responsibility of Business Is to

Increase Profits," the *New York Times*.

Goleman, D. (1998). *Working With Emotional Intelligence*, Bantam-Dell, NY.

Herzberg, F. (1966). *Work and the Nature of Man*, World Publishing, NY.

Jones, G. R. (2013). *Organization Theory, Design, and Change*, Pearson, NY.

Katz, D., and R. Kahn. (1966). *The Social Psychology of Organizations*, John Wiley & Sons, Inc., NY.

Kirkman, B. L., Gibson, C. B. & D. L. Shapiro. (2001). "Exporting Teams: Enhancing the Implementation and Effectiveness of Work Teams in Global Abilities,", *Organization Dynamics*, NY.

Kolb, D. (2007). *Kolb Learning Style Inventory*, Hay Group, USA.

Kolditz, T. (2007). *In Extremis Leadership: Leading as if Your Life Depended on It*, John Wiley & Sons.

Larkey, P. D. & L. S. Sproule. (1984). *Advances in Information Processing in Organizations*, JAI Press, CT.

Lindblom, C. E. (1959). "The Science of Muddling Through," *Public Administration Review*.

Luthans, F., Luthans, K. & B. Luthans. (2004). "Positive Psychological Capital: Beyond Human and Social Capital," *Business Horizons*, vol. 47, issue 1.

Maples, M. F. (1988). "Group Development: Extending Tuckman's Theory," *Journal for Specialists in Group Work.*

Mintzberg, H., Raisinghani, D. & Theoret (1976). "The Structure of Unstructured Decision-Making," *Administrative Science Quarterly.*

Myers, I., McCauley, M., Quenk, N. & A. Hammer. (1998). *MBTI Manual*, Consulting Psychologist Press USA.

Odiorne, George S. (1965). *Management by Objectives*, Pitman Publishing Corp, NY.

Pondy, L. R. (1967). "Organizational Conflict: Concepts and Models," *Administrative Science Quarterly.*

Sapolsky, R. (2010). "Why Zebras Don't Get Ulcers," Stanford Executive Briefing-DVD, CA.

Schein, E. (1969). *Process Consultation*, Addison-Wesley, MA.

Schein, E. (2006). *Career Anchors*, Pfeiffer, CA.

Simon, M. A. (1960). *The New Science of Management Decision*, Harper & Row, NY.

Skinner, B. F. (1971). *Contingencies of Reinforcement*, Appleton Century-Crofts, CT.

Vaill, P. B. (1982). "The purposing of high-performing systems," *Organization Dynamics*, NY.

Vroom, V. (1964). *Work and Motivation*, John Wiley & Sons, Inc., NY.

Vitters, A. & N. Kinzer. (1977). "Report of the Admission of Women to the U.S. Military Academy" (Project Athena), USMA Technical Report.

Vitters, A. G. (1978). "Motivation," *Infantry*, Mar–Apr.

Vitters, A. G. (1987). "Teamwork and Synchronization: Blitzkrieg of the '80s," *Armor*, Jul–Aug.

Vitters, A. G. (1983). "Command and Control on the Modern Battlefield," *Army Organization Effectiveness Journal*, No. 3–4.

About the Author

Al Vitters was born in Brooklyn and raised in Northport (LI), NY. He graduated from the U.S. Military Academy (West Point) in 1968 and served in the U.S. Army for 24 years before retiring as a Colonel. He was assigned to command and staff positions, including two combat tours in Vietnam, four years in Germany, and a year in Panama. In addition, he served on the faculty at West Point with the Dept. of Behavioral Sciences and Leadership.

Alan G. Vitters

He holds MS and PhD degrees from the University of Utah. He has taught management-related courses for Embry-Riddle Aeronautical University, the University of North Florida, and, more recently, at St. Joseph's College. He has also conducted and published research in leadership, motivation theory, and organizational change and development, to include Project Athena- a pioneering study of women at West Point (1977)

He and his wife, Kathy, have one son, a daughter-in-law, and three grandchildren. They enjoy travel, the theater, and contributing to local civic and veterans' groups. They currently reside in Ft. Salonga, NY.

CPSIA information can be obtained
at www.ICGtesting.com
Printed in the USA
LVHW041757150523
747056LV00013B/145